Realms Unwritten: Boundless Buccaneers

A Visual Writing Prompt Book for Students, Creatives, and Authors

D. B. Hopson

FORD MOUNTAIN PUBLISHING, LLC

Paperback ISBN: 979-8-89552-015-4

Cover Design by D. B. Hopson.

Art prompted in Midjourney and edited by D. B. Hopson.

Ford Mountain Publishing, LLC formatted and edited this book. Ford Mountain Publishing is a veteran-owned, family-run independent publisher dedicated to bringing imaginative stories to life. We specialize in crafting engaging fiction, beautifully illustrated books, and unique storytelling experiences that inspire readers of all ages. We also work closely with non-profit organizations to produce non-fiction pieces crafted to edify and encourage.

Contents

Introduction

How to Use a Prompt Book (If This Is Your First Time)

Each picture in this book was chosen in the hope that it will stir something in you—salt air in your lungs, wind in your hair, a flicker of curiosity, a question that won't sit still.

"Stir what?" you might ask.

Wonder. Emotion. A restless pull toward a horizon not yet reached.

You see a ship cutting across open water. Where is she bound? What cargo does she carry—spices, silver, stolen letters, something far more dangerous? You glimpse a jungle shore. Who waits beyond the tree line? Is there gold buried in those hills? A curse sealed in a forgotten chest? A bargain struck under a blood-red sunset?

Make it up—then write it down. **Bam**. That's a story. *Bada bing, bada boom*—you've got yourself a mutiny in the making, a desperate chase, a piece of flash fiction, or the first brick in a sprawling world no one else has ever seen. Only you, the author, know what truly lies beyond the frame.

It may surprise you how easily you are carried away by the creak of timbers and the snap of canvas sails. This is a good thing. The sea has always carried those willing to step aboard.

When you look at the pictures, ask yourself what isn't shown. What happened five minutes before this moment? What disaster—or triumph—comes five minutes after? Why does the captain never remove their gloves? What secret does the smuggler keep? Who truly owns the treasure?

You might wonder whether all these images belong to the same ocean, the same world, the same legendary pirate's long career. I don't know. That's for you to decide.

Are these fragments from rival captains' journals? Tavern tales whispered from Tortuga to Port Royal? Fever dreams?

Stand-alone snippets of make-believe places and times? Or one grand saga stitched together across continents and years?

If you want to connect them all, you can. If you want them to stand alone, you can do that too. Or chart a course somewhere in between. Let your imagination run wild. The wind favors the bold.

While space has been outlined for you on the page, you are always welcome—encouraged, even—to continue your tale elsewhere if you run out of room. Running out of space is a fine problem to have. It means the voyage has grown larger than the harbor provided.

Grab pen and paper. Open a blank document. Hoist your sails and keep going.

Why does this matter?

Because once upon a time, we all stood at the edge of imaginary seas without hesitation. As children, we declared couches to be ships and living rooms to be storm-tossed waters. Curiosity was our compass. Wonder was our north star.

Over time, the world hands us maps already drawn. It tells us which routes are safe. Which dreams are practical. Which answers are correct. We grow cautious. We fear being wrong.

We fear looking foolish. We learn not to "make things up." But fiction isn't lying—it's exploration.

No ship ever discovered a new world by hugging the shore.

That small voice inside you—the one that feels restless when routine grows too tight—that's your neglected creativity tapping at the hull, asking to set sail. It's easy to drift, to consume endless distraction like a sailor becalmed. It is much harder—and much braver—to create.

What value does a made-up story hold? I might ask you what work is done when you lift weights at the gym. The value is in the exercise. In the strengthening. In the daring.

Writing is the practice of thinking. It forces you to decide: Who betrays whom? Who keeps their oath? Who pays the price? It sharpens your mind and stretches your courage.

Reading is a voyage guided by another captain. (And I love reading—you should too.) Writing is when you take the helm yourself. Your stories may be silly or serious. Brutal or hopeful. Filled with roaring broadsides or quiet conversations beneath starlight. Just create.

And if you're shy about sharing what you write, that's perfectly fine. Many authors sail under borrowed names. You have that right as well.

As for the captions beneath the images: they exist only to offer a gentle nudge if you find yourself staring at a still sea. Ignore them if you wish. Rewrite them. Defy them.

These are your waters now. And any instructions I've given? Treat them like the Pirate Code—more like guidelines, really.

For centuries, pirates have haunted the edges of history—sometimes villains, sometimes folk heroes, always larger than life. The Age of Sail was a time of thunderous cannons, fragile alliances, whispered mutinies, and maps that left dangerous blanks where certainty should have been.

Stories about pirates have always captured imaginations. Perhaps the tales you've read—or watched—sparked your interest in the first place. Stories have a way of doing that.

But the best pirate story—the one you will like most—hasn't been written yet. Because it's the one you're about to write.

It will have all the elements you love: the right balance of danger and daring, treasure and treachery, loyalty and betrayal, freedom and cost. What does your captain truly seek? Gold? Revenge? Redemption? A place to belong? Only you can decide.

Step aboard this swashbuckling edition of *Realms Unwritten*, chart your course, and discover the stories waiting just beyond the horizon.

A boy and his treasure

Many young boys dream of being pirates, but Tommy became a pirate when...

To see the horizon

From the tops of the cliff, he could see...

A rogue's letter

To my dearest mother...

The pirate oasis

The map claimed treasure was beneath the hut, but the real secret was...

A pirate's wardrobe choice

Eric always wore a red shirt and brown pants to battle because...

The clothes make the man

What information is this pirate trying to acquire in town while blending in?

Disaster in the lagoon

The lagoon was too shallow for escape, and the flames were spreading faster than the tide...

A captain's tale

What sort of tale is this captain about to tell you?

The piratess

She stood where most quaked, ready for anything. Anything, that is, except…

Ruminating on the ramparts

Somewhere beyond the horizon lay the object that consumed his thoughts...

The privateer's contract

What sort of document is he signing that has them all so inter-ested?

The mapmaker

He smiled faintly when the stranger approached, already aware
of the question...

The seaborn chase

"Yep, that's me. You are probably wondering how we ended up here. Well..."

A map's story

They all were asking the same question. 'Is this map really to the buried treasure of...'

The captain's daughter

She dressed to match the love of her life, the sea, not caring that...

The Crown's agent

He waited patiently. At any moment now he was expecting a visitor, come to tell him about...

A shocking discovery

This paper contradicted everything the captain had told them. How will they respond?

One man's treasure

The chest looked full, but his knife hit something strange. It was...

Clapped in irons

He had been captured, or rescued, depending on who told the story.

Waiting for adventure

He looked like a man wasting time, which was exactly the disguise he needed while...

The traitor's interrogation

He refused to answer, not because he was loyal, but because the truth too dangerous to reveal to them. What did he know?

Marooned

Survival would depend on whether they trusted each other. But trust was hard to come by when...

The forger and the rogue

The pirate watched her pen move wishing he could read. What was she writing?

A wee night cap

He had left that life behind, but was it worth it?

Deathly treasure

After finding the treasure, he couldn't help but wonder if it truly contained everything he'd hoped for.

About the Creator

D.B. Hopson is a born storyteller who inherited the gift from his father. He was the first in his kindergarten class to conquer the mystery of shoe-tying—and he's been unstoppable ever since (just ask his Marine buddies!). D.B. Hopson loves spinning tall tales at storytelling guilds and gatherings, and he stays busy working with the family business, Ford Mountain Publishing, LLC, and in chasing down his daughter, who has taken after him in wanting to go fast! If you meet him, be sure to ask about Lord of the Rings lore or his favorite dinosaur!

⊙
instagram.com/hopson_daniel

in
linkedin.com/in/danielhopson45/

www.ingramcontent.com/pod-product-compliance
Lightning Source LLC
Chambersburg PA
CBHW051647120626
46551CB00015B/2254